NATIONAL
GEOGRAPHIC

GOING UP THE MOUNTAIN

David Tunkin

CONTENTS

This is a tall mountain.

Life at the top of the mountain is very different from life at the base, or bottom, of the mountain.

THE BASE OF THE MOUNTAIN

At the base of the mountain it is warm.

People live here.

rabbit

deer

badger

ferns

Many animals live at the base of the mountain.

Rabbits, deer, and badgers live here.

Many plants grow at the base of the mountain.

Flowers and ferns grow here.

THE MOUNTAIN FOREST

As you go up the mountain, it starts to get cooler.

Many trees grow in the forest here.

Evergreen and aspen trees grow thick and tall.

porcupine

beaver

snowshoe hare

wolves

bears

Beavers, porcupines, and snowshoe hares all live in the mountain forest.

Wolves and bears live here, too.

woodpecker

owl

Many birds live in the mountain forest.
Woodpeckers and owls live here.

ABOVE THE TIMBERLINE

As you go further up the mountain, it gets cooler still.

Soon there are no more trees.

This is called the timberline.

Trees do not grow above the timberline.

15

moss

Mosses and grasses grow above the timberline.

They grow in mountain meadows.

Little flowers grow in the meadows in spring.

mountain goat

pika

chipmunks

Different animals live above the timberline.

Mountain goats, pikas, and chipmunks all live here.

They eat the mosses and grasses.

ABOVE THE SNOWLINE

As you go further up the mountain, it gets colder.

There is always ice and snow on the ground here.

This is called the snowline.

Animals cannot live above the snowline.

Plants cannot grow here.

It is very cold and windy at the top of the mountain.

23

GLOSSARY

fern   plant with feathery leaves and no flowers

forest   land covered with trees and other plants

meadow   land with grass on it

moss   plant that grows in damp places

mountain   very high hill

snowline   the line marking the area where ice and snow
                never melt on the top of a mountain

timberline the line marking where trees stop growing on
                the side of a mountain